*The Sayings of C*

*The Sayings of*

# CHARLOTTE BRONTË

edited by

T.J. Winnifrith

DUCKWORTH

First published in 1996 by
Gerald Duckworth & Co. Ltd.
The Old Piano Factory
48 Hoxton Square, London N1 6PB
Tel: 0171 729 5986
Fax: 0171 729 0015

Introduction and editorial arrangement
© 1996 by T.J. Winnifrith

All rights reserved. No part of this publication
may be reproduced, stored in a retrieval system, or
transmitted, in any form or by any means, electronic,
mechanical, photocopying, recording or otherwise,
without the prior permission of the publisher.

A catalogue record for this book is available
from the British Library

ISBN 0 7156 2744 9

Typeset by Ray Davies
Printed in Great Britain by
Redwood Books Ltd, Trowbridge

# Contents

# Introduction

Of all the people in Duckworth's interesting series Jane Austen is obviously easiest to relate to Charlotte Brontë. She is English, a woman, a novelist writing in the nineteenth century, a daughter of a clergyman. Both Austen and Brontë were precocious writers in their youth, both wrote interesting letters, fortunately preserved though with some difficulty, both died sadly early leaving as their legacy a few novels which have been hard to dislodge from the canon of English literature. It is not surprising that in making my selection of the sayings of Charlotte Brontë I have modelled myself fairly shamelessly on the admirable *Sayings of Jane Austen*, edited by Maggie McKernan.

But Austen and Brontë are not sisters under the same skin. Austen died in 1817, Brontë was born in 1816. The end of the French Revolution and the beginning of the Industrial Revolution affected the two writers in different ways. So too did the rise of the Romantic movement in poetry and art, the growth of Evangelicism within and outside the Church of England, the difference between the North and South of England, and above all the different circumstances of the Austen and Brontë families. Jane Austen's mother was related to the nobility, she had one very rich brother, two other brothers who became admirals, and was in a way a member of the Establishment. Charlotte Brontë's father began life as an Irish peasant earning his way through piety and hard work to a respectable marriage and a respectable post as permanent curate of Haworth, but he did not exactly become a member of the gentry, in spite of falsely claiming aristocratic ancestry and connections. Charlotte's relations lived a long way away in Ireland and in Cornwall. She did not have many friends, and her brothers and sisters were sources of anxiety rather than support. There would have been little money left to the Brontës if their father had died, and they would have had to earn their living in the friendless world of the governess. There is none of this precarious existence in the life of Jane Austen, surrounded by relatives and friends, not surrounded by financial worries, although of course she had her troubles. Oddly in a rather neat but tragic reversal Austen was the first member of her immediate family to die, apart from her father, predeceasing her mother, six brothers and a sister, whereas Charlotte was predeceased by her mother, four sisters and a brother, leaving her lonely father to mourn her when she died in 1855.

These biographical details may not interest those who see Austen and Brontë as novelists of love and marriage. The most famous saying of Austen is probably the opening sentence of the first chapter of her most famous novel, 'It is a truth, universally acknowledged that a single man in possession of a fortune must be in need of a wife'. The most famous saying of Brontë is almost certainly 'Reader, I married him', although the earlier 'Reader, I forgave him at the moment, and on the spot', must be a close second. Unfortunately Mr Rochester, though he has a fortune, is not a single man, and therefore needs more forgiveness than Darcy and needs the death of Mrs Rochester before he can be married. But this is not the only reason why 'Pride and Mr Rochester' or 'Elizabeth Eyre' cannot be written. We must see a change from the confidence of universal acknowledgement to the boldly nervous address to the reader.

One reason for this change lies again in the personal circumstances of each writer. Austen did not marry, although she had her fair share of proposals, was known for her flirtatiousness in her youth, and was able to observe the effects of love and marriage among her friends and relations. Remarkably four of her brothers married twice, whereas Charlotte was the only member of her family to marry, and that only after she had virtually completed her writing career. But of course she had proposals and a love affair, if it can be so called, with a married man, her schoolmaster in Belgium, and she put this love affair in her novels, whose heroes turn out to be married men or Belgians or schoolmasters or a combination of these desirable attributes. Austen is less autobiographical. She is not more circumspect about extra-marital affairs, which are treated with a brisk and sensible condemnation, whereas Brontë regards them with fascinated horror. This difference is partly due to the onset of Victorian prudery, partly due to personal circumstances. The lack of passion in Austen's novels which Brontë so roundly condemned is probably due to a difference in temperaments; if alive Austen would have condemned Brontë for a lack of taste.

In *Pride and Prejudice* Darcy tells Elizabeth Bennet that she is humble and insignificant, and understandably she rejects him, although a visit to the orderly world of Pemberley and acknowledgement of Darcy's virtues makes her change her mind. In *Jane Eyre* Rochester tells Jane she is humble and insignificant, and she falls into his arms, although the presence of the first Mrs Rochester causes a change of heart. When Rochester does eventually marry he is humbled and blinded, while Jane has discovered some quite grand relations and five thousand pounds. Both Austen and Brontë have been accused of being both snobbish and mercenary. It has been said of Austen's novels that she insists that it is wicked to marry for money, but foolish to marry without it. Brontë is always talking about the need for a competence. Austen is rather contemptuous of the vulgar Miss Steeles and the pretentious Mrs Elton. Brontë is at pains to stress Crimsworth's Etonian education, the ancient lineage of Mr Rochester and the Rivers family, Shirley's superiority to her suitors, and even poor Lucy Snowe's aristocratic-sounding uncles. Snobbery is of course fairly silly. Neither birth nor wealth is any substitute for worth, as Austen recognises when she contrasts the admirable Admiral Croft with the pathetic Sir Walter Elliot, despising Mrs Smith yet fawning on the honourable Miss Carteret. Brontë, coming from a less confident background, is perhaps on less sure ground when she criticizes the house party at Thornfield Hall for their aristocratic airs and graces, showing herself very ignorant of the aristocracy, while she criticises the Belgian aristocracy in *Villette* for not being aristocratic enough. Her attacks on the vulgar Sam Wynne and her plebeian employers the Whites together with Crimsworth's and Lucy Snowe's attitude to their rich pupils can be seen as the personal cry of despair of an educated governess resentful of the way in which she was neglected and despised by those rich enough to employ her, but not clever enough to appreciate her.

Brontë was both clever and educated, although educated in the rather old fashioned way that girls were taught in the early nineteenth century. Like her heroine Frances Henri, and indeed like many intellectuals, she was better at learning than teaching, and critical of the schools at which she was taught and at which she taught. Brontë was not suited to be a teacher; her shyness, her size, her dislike of her pupils and her eagerness for the truth were obstacles to success in a profession which demands enthusiasm or the pretence of it. But in both fact and fiction Brontë had many interesting things to say on teachers and education, and perhaps like Frances Henri and Lucy Snowe she might have made a good headmistress if she had been given the opportunity.

The Brontë household was a religious one, and in an Evangelical way was not afraid of showing this in a manner totally alien to the polite reticence of Austen, whose religion, though genuine, is rarely revealed in her letters or her novels. It is hard to remember that Henry Tilney and Edward Ferrars are clergymen, while Mr Collins and Mr Elton show the clergy in a poor light. Brontë's clergymen are generally a bad lot. Mr Brocklehurst is a bully, St John Rivers lacks human warmth, and the curates in *Shirley* are fools, while non-conformists and Roman Catholics are shown to be wicked. And yet all Brontë's heroines are guided by a Divine purpose, as she makes clear on a number of occasions.

Austen, apart from the famous remark about a little bit of ivory, is reticent about the books she read and her own mode of writing. She does by implication criticize the Gothic novel when she makes Catherine Morland work herself into a frenzy over a laundry list and attacks novels full of coincidence when in a juvenile work she suddenly throws a whole set of relations together. Brontë's novels are full of Gothic extravagances and coincidences, and one can't help feeling that Austen would have been as harsh on Brontë as Brontë was on her. Brontë does have something to say about her writing and is full of information about her reading. Brontë was also a painter, as indeed were all her family and some of her heroines; her books are full of information about pictures and pictures in words. Austen wrote before the Romantic movement had became respectable; there are some slightly snide remarks about Captain Benwick's fondness for Byron, but nature does not play much part in Austen's world whereas it is clearly very important for Brontë's lonely heroines, imbued with the romanticism which unites Wordsworth and Byron.

This is a book about Charlotte Brontë, but it seemed rather churlish to omit other members of her family, whose tragic deaths left a mark on Charlotte. I have selected a few typical sayings of Anne, Branwell and Emily, and their father and mother. It would have been tempting to add a few comments from other people about Charlotte, whom Thackeray and Matthew Arnold found so formidable and Mrs Gaskell so pathetic, but this would hardly be fair in a series of sayings by particular individuals. Indeed it could be a criticism of my selection that many of the quotations are not particularly interesting in themselves, but are more interesting for what they say about the author. But Brontë wrote about herself in a way that Austen would have thought selfish, and so it is useful to know how her mind worked. Unlike Austen, Brontë wrote about subjects of which she knew little, such as the aristocracy and masculine conversation; this gives some of her sayings a slightly ridiculous air until we realize that it is the author who is still speaking to us even in a rather absurd charade. Brontë makes Rochester sing to Jane a song about his lawless love; she had previously written a poem with a strongly autobiographical air in which a pupil talks about her lawless love for her teacher.

\*

I have taken quotations from the novels from the Clarendon edition. Unfortunately the imminent edition of Brontë correspondence in this series was not available when I made my selection, and I have had to rely on the Shakespeare Head edition. The juvenilia have only been partly edited in a proper fashion, but I have not found much of interest either in them or the poems. In trying to put the sayings in chronological order I have taken July 1846 as the date for *The Professor*, August 1847 as the date for *Jane Eyre*, August 1849 as the date for *Shirley*, and December 1852 as the date for *Villette*, as these are the months in which Brontë completed her manuscripts, although *The Professor* was later revised and not published until 1857.

I have indicated the speaker or speakers in round brackets in the attribution and the person spoken about in square brackets in the quotation. In *Jane Eyre*, *The Professor* and *Villette* the narrators (Jane Eyre, Crimsworth and Lucy Snowe) have voices that are sometimes difficult to disentangle from the voices of these characters.

# Love

The combat betwixt true love and duty raged for a few seconds in the Marquis's heart and sent his life-blood in a tumult of agony and despair, burning to his cheek and brow.

Juvenile Manuscript, 20 August 1832

Unloved I love, unwept I weep,
Grief I restrain, hope I repress;
Vain is this anguish, fixed and deep,
Vainer desires or dreams of bliss.

Poem, *c*. 1836

'Will you be my mistress –?' 'No.' 'You said you adored me.' 'I do, intensely – but I'll never be your mistress.'

(Sir William Percy and Elizabeth Hastings),
Juvenile Manuscript, 26 March 1839

But once a year he heard a whisper low and dreary
Appealing for aid, entreating some reply;
Only when sick, soul-worn, and torture-weary,
Breathed I that prayer, heaved I that sigh.

Poem, *c*. 1845

If my master withdraws his friendship entirely from me I shall be altogether without hope – if he gives me a little – just a little – I shall be satisfied – happy; I shall have reason for living on, for working.

Letter (original in French) to M. Heger, 8 January 1845

> His coming was my hope each day,
> His parting was my pain.
> The chance that did his steps delay
> Was ice in every vein.
>
> I gave entire affection now,
> I gave devotion sure,
> And strong took root and fast did grow
> One mighty feeling more.

Poem, c. 1845

I hated his fashion of mentioning Love, I abhorred, from my soul, mere Licentiousness. [M. Pelet]

The Professor, 8

I hate boldness – that boldness which is of the brassy brow and insensate nerves; but I love the courage of the strong heart, the fervour of the generous blood.

Ibid., 19

> I gave, at first, Attention close;
> Then interest warm ensued;
> From interest, as improvement rose,
> Succeeded gratitude.

(Frances Henri), Ibid., 23

Yet, whereas one moment I was sitting solus on the chair near the table, the next I held Frances on my knee, placed there with sharpness and decision, and retained with exceeding tenacity.          *Ibid.*

It appeared, then, that I too was a sensualist, in my temperate and fastidious way.          *Ibid.*

'You never felt jealousy, did you, Miss Eyre? Of course not: I need not ask you; because you never felt love. You have both sentiments yet to experience: your soul sleeps; the shock is yet to be given which shall waken it.'

(Mr Rochester), Jane Eyre, I,15

Till morning dawned I was tossed on a buoyant but unquiet sea, where billows of trouble rolled under surges of joy.

*Ibid.*

Never had he called me more frequently to his presence; never been kinder to me when there – and, alas! never had I loved him so well.

*Ibid.*, II,7

> 'Her coming was my hope each day,
> Her parting was my pain;
> The chance that did her steps delay
> Was ice in every vein.'

(Mr Rochester), *Ibid.*, II,9

My future husband was becoming to me my whole world; and more than the world: almost my hope of heaven. He stood between me and every thought of religion, as an eclipse intervenes between man and the broad sun. I could not, in those days, see God for His creature: of whom I had made an idol.

*Ibid.*

Reader, I forgave him at the moment and on the spot.

*Ibid.*, III,1

'You shall be Mrs Rochester – both virtually and nominally. I shall keep only to you so long as you and I live. You shall go to a place I have in the south of France: a white-walled villa on the shores of the Mediterranean. There you shall live a happy, and guarded, and most innocent life. Never fear that I wish to lure you into error – to make you my mistress.'

(Mr Rochester), *Ibid.*

'I sought my ideal of a woman amongst English ladies, French comtesses, Italian signoras, and German Gräfinnen. I could not find her.'

(Mr Rochester), *Ibid.*

'It is strange,' pursued he, 'that while I love Rosamund Oliver so wildly – with all the intensity, indeed, of a first passion, the object of which is exquisitely beautiful, graceful, and fascinating – I experience at the same time a calm, unwarped consciousness that she would not make me a good wife.'

(St John Rivers), *Ibid.*, III,6

And it was the voice of a human being – a known, loved, well-remembered voice – that of Edward Fairfax Rochester; and it spoke in pain and woe, wildly, eerily, urgently.

*Ibid.*, III,9

He is not my husband, nor ever will be. He does not love me: I do not love him. [St John Rivers]

*Ibid.*, III,11

Love is stronger than Cruelty, stronger than Death, but perishes under Meanness; Pity may take its place, but Pity is not Love.

Letter to W.S. Williams, 1 May 1848

A lover masculine so disappointed can speak and urge explanation; a lover feminine can say nothing; if she did, the result would be shame and anguish, inward remorse for self-treachery.

*Shirley*, I,7

'Indisputably, a great, good, handsome man is the first of created things.'

(Shirley Keeldar), *Ibid.*, II,1

'Robert is a first-rate man – in my eyes. I *have* loved, *do* love, and *must* love him. I would be his wife if I could; as I cannot, I must go where I shall never see him.'

(Caroline Helstone), *Ibid.*, II,3

Let me be content with a temperate draught of this living stream: let me not run athirst, and apply passionately to its welcome waters: let me not imagine in them a sweeter taste than earth's fountains know.

*Villette*, 16

'Ginevra!' He thought her so fair, so good; he spoke so lovingly of her charms, her sweetness, her innocence, that in spite of my plain prose knowledge of the reality, a kind of reflected glow began to settle on her idea, even for me. [John Bretton]

*Ibid.*, 18

I took my letter, trembling with sweet impatience; I broke its seal.
'Will it be long – will it be short?'

*Ibid.*, 22

'Lived and loved!' said she, 'is that the summit of earthly happiness, the end of life – to love?'

(Polly Hume), *Ibid.*, 26

'Good-night, Dr. John; you are good, you are beautiful; but you are not mine. Good-night, and God bless you!'

(Lucy Snowe), *Ibid.*, 31

'Lucy, take my love. One day share my life. Be my dearest, first on earth.'

(Paul Emanuel), *Ibid.*, 41

Shaking from head to foot, looking deadly pale, speaking low, vehemently yet with difficulty – he made me for the first time feel what it costs a man to declare affection when he doubts response. [Mr Nicholls]

Letter to Ellen Nussey, 15 December 1852

Without loving him, I don't like to think of him suffering in solitude. [Mr Nicholls]

Letter to Ellen Nussey, 2 January 1853

I know what *love* is as I understand it.

Letter to Harriet Martineau, 1853

It is a solemn and strange and perilous thing for a woman to become a wife.

Letter to Ellen Nussey, 9 August 1854

I find in my husband the tenderest nurse, the kindest support – the best earthly comfort that ever woman had.

Letter to Ellen Nussey, 21 February 1855

# Marriage

O Zamorna, do take pity on me! Forgive me this once! If I had known, if I had in the faintest degree imagined that one hair of my husband's noble head could have been injured by what I did, I would rather have cut off my right hand than stirred a step on that cursed journey.

(Mary Percy), *The Spell: An Extravaganza*, 1834

Before the honeymoon was well ended, Julia began to find out the worth of her bargain, and Sydney perceived that accomplished, lovely and high-born as his bride was, she had never been intended by nature to sympathise or amalgamate with him.

*The Scrap Book*, 1835

Do not therefore accuse me of wrong motives when I say that my answer to your proposal must be a *decided negative*.

Letter to Henry Nussey, 5 March 1839

It proved to be a declaration of attachment and proposal of Matrimony, expressed in the ardent language of the sapient young Irishman. [Mr Pryce]

Letter to Ellen Nussey, 4 August 1839

Do not be over-persuaded to marry a man you can never respect – I do not say *love*, because, I think, if you can respect a person before marriage, moderate love at least will come after; and as to intense *passion*, I am convinced that this is no desirable feeling.

Letter to Ellen Nussey, 15 May 1840

But it is an imbecility, which I reject with contempt, for women, who have neither fortune nor beauty, to make marriage the principal object of their wishes and hopes, and the aim of all their actions.

Letter to Ellen Nussey, 1 April 1843

I know that if women wish to escape the stigma of husband-seeking they must act and look like marble or clay – cold, expressionless, bloodless; for every appearance of feeling, of joy, sorrow, friendliness, antipathy, admiration, disgust are alike construed by the world into an attempt to hook a husband.

Letter to Ellen Nussey, 2 April 1845

'Marry! Will birds pair? Of course it is both her intention and resolution to marry when she finds a suitable match, and no one is better aware than herself of the sort of impression she is capable of producing.'

(M. Pelet on Mdlle Reuter), *The Professor*, 11

The idea of marrying a doll or a fool was always abhorrent to me; I know that a pretty doll, a fair fool, might do well enough for the honeymoon; but when passion cooled, how dreadful to find a lump of wax and wood laid in my bosom, a half idiot clasped in my arms, and to remember that I had made of this my equal – nay my idol.                                    *Ibid.*, 12

Reason was my physician. She began by proving that the prize I had missed was of little value; she admitted that, physically, Zoraide might have suited me, but affirmed that our souls were not in harmony, and that discord must have resulted from the union of her mind and mine.

*Ibid.*, 13

We took no bridal trip; our modesty, screened by the peaceful obscurity of our station and the pleasant isolation of our circumstances, did not exact that additional precaution.                          *Ibid.*, 25

Monsieur, if a wife's nature loathes that of the man she is wedded to, marriage must be slavery. *Ibid.*

Who gravely asked you whether Miss Brontë was not going to be married to her Papa's Curate?

Letter to Ellen Nussey, 10 July 1846

Besides, no husband ought to be an object of charity to his wife – as no wife to her husband.

Letter to Ellen Nussey, 9 August 1846

I saw he was going to marry her, for family, perhaps political reasons, because her rank and connections suited him. [Mr Rochester and Blanche Ingram]

*Jane Eyre*, II,2

'My bride! What bride? I have no bride!'

(Mr Rochester), *Ibid.*, II,8

'My bride is here,' he said, again drawing me to him, 'because my equal is here, and my likeness, Jane, will you marry me?'

(Mr Rochester), *Ibid.*

'You – you strange, you almost unearthly thing! – I love as my own flesh. You – poor and obscure, and small and plain as you are – I entreat to accept me as a husband.'

(Mr Rochester), *Ibid.*

'The marriage cannot go on: I declare the existence of an impediment.'

(Mr Briggs) *Ibid.*, II,11

'That is *my wife*', said he. 'Such is the sole conjugal embrace I am ever to know – such are the endearments which are to solace my leisure hours!'

(Mr Rochester on Bertha Mason), *Ibid.*

'I lived with that woman upstairs four years, and before that time she had tried me indeed.'

(Mr Rochester on Bertha Mason), *Ibid.*, III,1

'How can I, a man not yet thirty, take out with me to
India a girl of nineteen, unless she be married to me?
How can we be for ever together – sometimes in
solitudes, sometimes amidst savage tribes – and unwed?'

(St John Rivers), *Ibid.*, III,8

No woman was ever nearer to her mate than I am: ever
more absolutely bone of his bone and flesh of his flesh.

*Ibid.*, III,12

'When people love, the next step is they marry.'

(Caroline Helstone), *Shirley*, I,7

'Millions of marriages are unhappy; if everybody
confessed the truth, perhaps all are more or less so.'

(Mr Helstone), *Ibid.*

'I think these are not times for marrying or giving in
marriage.'

(Robert Moore), *Ibid.*, I,9

'Probably I shall be an old maid.'

(Caroline Helstone), *Ibid.*, I,10

'Leading and improving! teaching and tutoring! bearing
and forbearing! Pah! my husband is not to be my baby.'

(Shirley Keeldar), *Ibid.*, III,13

'Oh could I find her such as I imagine her! Something to
tame first, and teach afterwards; to break in and then to
fondle.'

(Louis Moore), *Ibid.*

I wish dear Ellen, you would tell me what is the
'twaddle about my marrying, etc.,' which you hear.

Letter to Ellen Nussey, 14 September 1850

Other reasons regulate matrimony – reasons of
convenience, of connection, of money. [George Smith]

Letter to Ellen Nussey, 20 January 1851

It would a more likely match if 'matches' were at all in question, which *they are not*. [James Taylor]

Letter to Ellen Nussey, 30 January 1851

Would Mr Taylor and I ever suit?

Letter to Ellen Nussey, 9 April 1851

*He* perhaps was not in love; but how many people ever *do* love, or at least marry for love, in this world? We waited the end. [Madame Beck and John Bretton]

*Villette*, 11

'No woman were she as beautiful as Aphrodite, who could give or receive such a glance, shall ever be sought in marriage by me.'

(John Bretton on Ginevra Fanshawe), *Ibid.*, 20

In fact, dear Ellen, I am engaged.

Letter to Ellen Nussey, 11 April 1854

My dear husband too, appears in a new light here in his own country.

Letter to Margaret Wooler, 10 July 1854

I believe my dear husband to be a good man, and trust I have done right.

Letter to Catherine Wooler, 18 July 1854

# Birth

Well can I believe that Mrs W. has been an exciseman's daughter, and I am convinced also that Mr W.'s extraction is very low.

Letter to Ellen Nussey, 4 May 1841

First, after leaving Eton, I had an interview with my maternal uncles, Lord Tynedale and the Hon. John Seacombe. *The Professor*, 1

The Hunsdens were of an old stem – and scornful as Yorke (such was my late interlocutor's name) professed to be of the advantages of birth, in his secret heart he well knew and fully appreciated the distinction his ancient if not high lineage conferred on him in a mushroom place like X——, concerning whose inhabitants it was proverbially said that not one in a thousand knew his own grandfather. *Ibid.*, 3

'Now, if you'd only an estate, and a mansion, and a park, and a title, how you could play the exclusive, maintain the rights of your class, train your tenantry in habits of respect to the peerage, oppose at every step the advancing power of the people, support your rotten order, and be ready for its sake to wade knee-deep in churls' blood.'

(Hunsden on William Crimsworth), *Ibid.*, 4

'Hypocrite and Twaddler! smooth-faced, snivelling Greasehorn!'

(Edward Crimsworth on William Crimsworth), *Ibid.*, 5

'Examine the footprints of our august aristocracy, see how they walk in blood, crushing hearts as they go.'

(Hunsden), *Ibid.*, 24

Your well-bred people appear to me (figuratively speaking) to walk on their heads.

Letter to Ellen Nussey, January 1847

That my father had been a poor clergyman; that my mother had married him against the wishes of her friends, who considered the match beneath her; that my grandfather Reed was so irritated at her disobedience, he cut her off without a shilling. *Jane Eyre*, I,3

'Am I right, Baroness Ingram of Ingram Park?'
'My lily-flower, you are right now, as always.'

(Blanche Ingram and her mother), *Ibid.*, II,2

I smiled as I unfolded it, and devised how I would teaze you about your aristocratic tastes, and your efforts to masque your plebeian bride in the attributes of a peeress.

*Ibid.*, II,10

There were mercantile families in the district boasting twice the income, but the Keeldars, by virtue of their antiquity, and their distinction of lords of the manor, took the predecence of all.

*Shirley*, I,11

'You scarsley ever see a fam'ly where a propa carriage or a reg'la butla is kep;'

(Mr Donne), *Ibid.*, II,4

'Many who think themselves refined ladies and gentlemen, and on whose lips the word "vulgarity" is for ever hovering, cannot mention "love" without betraying their own innate and imbecile degradation.'

(Caroline Helstone), *Ibid.*, II,6

There is nothing the lower orders like better than a little downright good-humoured rating.

*Ibid.*, II,9

'All ridiculous irrational crying up of one class, whether
the same be aristocrat or democrat – all howling down of
another class, whether clerical or military – all exacting
justice to individuals, whether monarch or mendicant –
is really sickening to me; all arraying of ranks against
ranks, all party hatreds, all tyrannies disguised as
liberties, I reject and wash my hands of.'

(Shirley Keeldar), *Ibid.*, II,10

'And we two set store by ancient blood? We have family
pride, though one of us at least is a republican?'

(Shirley Keeldar), *Ibid.*

'The daughters of tradespeople, however well educated,
must necessarily be underbred, and as such unfit to be
inmates of OUR dwellings, or guardians of OUR children's
minds and persons.'

(Miss Hardman), *Ibid.*

'He has twice your money – twice your common sense –
equal connections – equal respectability.'

(Mr Sympson on Sam Wynne), *Ibid.*, III,4

'His intellect reaches no standard I can esteem: there is a
second stumbling-block. His views are narrow; his
feelings are blunt; his tastes are coarse; his manners
vulgar.'

(Shirley Keeldar on Sam Wynne), *Ibid.*

'Neither his title, wealth, pedigree, nor poetry avail to
invest him with the power I describe.'

(Shirley Keeldar on Sir Philip Nunnely), *Ibid.*, III,8

'I dare him to speak! the beggar! the knave! the specious
hypocrite! the vile, insinuating, infamous menial!;
Stand apart from my niece, sir; Let her go!'

(Mr Sympson on Louis Moore), *Ibid.*, III,13

He was a true young English gentleman. [John Bretton]
*Villette*, 7

'I suppose you are nobody's daughter.'
(Ginevra Fanshawe on Lucy Snowe), *Ibid.*, 14

'If this were not one of the compact little minor
European courts, whose very formalities are little more
imposing than familiarities, and whose grandeur is but
homeliness in Sunday array, it would sound all very
fine.'
(John Bretton), *Ibid.*, 20

# Wealth

A COMPETENCY WAS WHAT I WANTED; a competency it was now my aim and resolve to secure; but never had I been farther from the mark.

*The Professor*, 20

M. Vandenhuten was rich, respected, and influential; I poor, despised, and powerless.

*Ibid.*, 22

Of course his debts had to be paid. [Branwell]

Letter to Ellen Nussey, 13 December 1846

Glad was I to get him out of the silk warehouse, and then out of a jeweller's shop: the more he bought me, the more my cheek burned with a sense of annoyance and degradation.

*Jane Eyre*, II,9

'You do not know what it is to possess, nor consequently enjoy wealth: you cannot form a notion of the importance twenty thousand pounds would give you; of the place it would enable you to take in society; of the prospects it would open to you;'

(St John Rivers), *Ibid.*, III,7

I have always been accustomed to think that the necessity of earning one's subsistence is not in itself an evil, but I feel it may become a heavy evil if health fails, if employment lacks, if the demand upon our efforts made by the weakness of others dependent upon us becomes greater than our strength suffices to answer.

Letter to W.S. Williams, 15 June 1848

'I should think I could very likely get a wife with a few thousands, who would suit both me and my affairs.'

(Mr Yorke on Robert Moore), *Shirley*, I,9

These classes certainly think too exclusively of making money: they are too oblivious of every national consideration but that of extending England's (i.e. their own) commerce.

*Ibid.*, I,10

'I can do a good deed with my cash. My thousand a year is not merely a matter of dirty bank-notes and jaundiced guineas.'

(Shirley Keeldar), *Ibid.*, II,2

'*You* want to make a speculation of me. You would immolate me to that mill, your Moloch!'

(Shirley Keeldar on Robert Moore), *Ibid.*, III,7

'Your god, sir, is the world.'

(Shirley Keeldar on Mr Sympson), *Ibid.*, III,8

However, £500 is not to be despised.

Letter to Margaret Wooler, 7 December 1852

Three times that afternoon I had given crowns where I should have given shillings; but I consoled myself with the reflection, 'It is the price of experience.'     *Villette*, 6

'I have got my portion!' she cried at once; (Ginevra ever stuck to the substantial; I always thought there was a good trading element in her composition, much as she scorned the 'bourgeoisie');

*Ibid.*, 41

# Teaching

Weary with a day's hard work, during which an unusual degree of stupidity has been displayed by my promising pupils.

Letter to Ellen Nussey, 1836

A private governess has no existence, is not considered as a living and rational being except as connected with the wearisome duties she has to fulfil.

Letter to Emily, 8 June 1839

Papa and aunt talk, by fits and starts, of our – *id est*, Emily, Anne, and myself – commencing a school.

Letter to Ellen Nussey, 19 July 1841

As soon as I can get an assurance of only *one* pupil – I will have cards of terms printed – and will commence the repairs necessary in the house.

Letter to Ellen Nussey, 20 July 1844

When I had brought down my lesson to the lowest level of my dullest pupil's capacity, when I had shown myself the mildest, the most tolerant of masters, a word of impertinence, a movement of disobedience, changed me at once into a despot.

*The Professor*, 7

Of character I should think she possessed but little, as her pupils seemed constantly *en révolte* against her authority. [Frances Henri]

*Ibid.*, 12

Her teachers did not love her, but they submitted because they were her inferiors in everything. [Mdlle Reuter]
*Ibid.*

'You have come in too late to receive a lesson to-day; try to be more punctual next time.'
(Crimsworth to Frances Henri), *Ibid.*, 13

Know, O incredulous Reader! that a master stands in a somewhat different relation towards a pretty, light-headed, probably ignorant girl to that occupied by a partner at a ball or a gallant on the promenade.
*Ibid.*, 14

There were only about a dozen of them, but they made as much noise as might have sufficed for fifty; they seemed very little under her control. Three or four at once assailed her with importune requirements; she looked harassed, she demanded silence, but in vain. [Frances Henri]
*Ibid.*, 15

She would trample on the feet of Humility, she would kneel at the feet of Disdain; she would meet Tenderness with secret contempt, Indifference she would woo with ceaseless assiduities. [Mdlle Reuter]
*Ibid.*

'Well, then, if ever you are the head of a large establishment, dismiss nobody.'
(Mdlle Reuter), *Ibid.*, 18

In the day-time my house and establishment were conducted by Madame the Directress, a stately and elegant woman, bearing much anxious thought on her large brow, much calculated dignity in her serious mien. [Frances Henri, now Mrs Crimsworth]
*Ibid.*, 25

'It is a village-school: your scholars will be only poor girls – cottagers' children – at the best, farmers' daughters. Knitting, sewing, reading, writing, ciphering, will be all you have to teach. What will you do with your accomplishments? What, with the largest portion of your mind – sentiments – tastes?'

(St John Rivers), *Jane Eyre*, III,4

These could already read, write, and sew; and to them I taught the elements of grammar, geography, history, and the finer kinds of needlework.

*Ibid.*, III,6

Those who would urge on governesses more acquirements, do not know the origin of their chief sufferings.

Letter to W.S. Williams, 12 May 1848

'Governesses' she observed, 'must ever be kept in a sort of isolation.' [Miss Hardman]

*Shirley*, II,10

Yes, Louis Moore was a satellite of the house of Sympson – connected, yet apart, ever attendant, ever distant.

*Ibid.*, III,3

She is very well treated for a governess – but wore the usual pale, despondent look of her class.

Letter to Ellen Nussey, 19 March 1850

I was told, too, that neither masters nor teachers were found fault with in that establishment; yet both masters and teachers were often changed; they vanished and others filled their places, none could explain how.

*Villette*, 8

She was of little use as far as communication of knowledge went, but for strict surveillance and maintenance of rules she was invaluable. [Mdlle St Pierre]

*Ibid.,* 14

I commenced my school; I worked – I worked hard. I deemed myself the steward of his property, and determined, God willing, to render a good account.

*Ibid.,* 42

# Education

I was twenty-six years old a week or two since, and at this ripe time of life I am a schoolgirl, a complete schoolgirl, and, on the whole, very happy in that capacity.                    Letter to Ellen Nussey, May 1842

'Do you know anything besides that useless trash of college learning, Greek, Latin and so forth?'
    'I have studied Mathematics.'
    'Stuff! I dare say you have.'
    'I can read and write French and German.'
                    (Edward and William Crimsworth), *The Professor*, 2

She liked to learn, but hated to teach. [Frances Henri]
                    *Ibid.*, 16

Victor learns fast. He must soon go to Eton, where, I suspect, his first year or two will be utter wretchedness.
                    *Ibid.*, 25

Again I reflected: I scarcely knew what school was; Bessie sometimes spoke of it as a place where young ladies sat in the stocks, wore back-boards, and were expected to be exceedingly genteel and precise.
                    *Jane Eyre*, I,3

Women are supposed to be very calm generally: but women feel just as men feel; they need exercise for their faculties, and a field for their efforts, as much as their brothers do; they suffer from too rigid a restraint, too absolute a stagnation, precisely as men would suffer; and it is narrow-minded in their more privileged fellow-creatures to say that they ought to confine themselves to making puddings and knitting stockings, to playing on the piano and embroidering bags.          *Ibid.*, I,12

'Put all crotchets out of your head, and run away and amuse yourself.'
  'What with? My doll?'

(Mr Helstone and Caroline Helstone), *Shirley*, I,11

'I long to have something absorbing and compulsory to fill my head and hands and to occupy my thoughts.'

(Caroline Helstone), *Ibid.*, II.1

It is permitted to a woman to teach and to exercise authority as much as may be.

(Caroline Helstone), *Ibid.*, II,7

Keep your girls' minds narrow and fettered – they will still be a plague and a care, sometimes a disgrace to you.

(Caroline Helstone), *Ibid.*, II,11

And if my Master has given me ten talents, my duty is to trade with them, and make them ten talents more. Not in the dust of household drawers shall the coin be interred.

(Rose Yorke), *Ibid.*, II,12

No women were educated in those days.

(Robert Moore), *Ibid.*, III,7

The girls of this generation have great advantages; it seems to me that they receive much encouragement in the acquisition of knowledge and the cultivation of their minds.

Letter to W.S. Williams, 19 March 1850

And then, in matters of information – in history, geography, arithmetic, and so on, I am quite a baby; and I write English so badly – such spelling and grammar, they tell me.

(Ginevra Fanshawe), *Villette*, 6

# The Church

He did not rant, he did not cant, he did not whine, he did not snivel, he just got up and spoke with the boldness of a man who was impressed with the truth of what he is saying, who has no fear of his enemies and no dread of consequences. [Mr Collins]

Letter to Ellen Nussey, 7 April 1840

I consider Methodism, Dissenterism, Quakerism, and the extremes of high and low Churchism foolish, but Roman Catholicism beats them all.

Letter to Ellen Nussey, July 1842

I took a fancy to change myself into a Catholic and go and make a real confession to see what it was like.

Letter to Emily, 2 September 1843

I think he must be like most other curates I have seen – and they seem to me a self-seeking, vain, empty race.

Letter to Ellen Nussey, 18 June 1845

A good clergyman is one of the best of men.

*The Professor*, 6

'I have a little boy, younger than you, who knows six Psalms by heart; and when you ask him which he would rather have, a gingerbread-nut to eat or a verse of a Psalm to learn, he says "Oh, the verse of a Psalm! Angels sing Psalms;" says he, "I wish to be a little angel here below"; he then gets two nuts in recompense for his infant piety.'

(Mr Brocklehurst), *Jane Eyre*, I,4

We set out cold, we arrived at church colder; during the morning service we became almost paralysed.

*Ibid.*, 1,7

'I have a Master to serve whose kingdom is not of this world: my mission is to mortify in these girls the lusts of the flesh; to teach them to clothe themselves with shame-facedness and sobriety, not with braided hair and costly apparel.'

(Mr Brocklehurst), *Ibid.*

'He that overcometh shall inherit all things; and I will be his God, and he shall be my son. But', was slowly, distinctly read, 'the fearful, the unbelieving etc., shall have their part in the lake which burneth with fire and brimstone, which is the second death.'

(St John Rivers), *Ibid.*, III,9

I love the Church of England. Her ministers, indeed, I do not regard as infallible personages.

Letter to W.S. Williams, 23 December 1847

Of late years, I say, an abundant shower of curates has fallen upon the north of England, but in eighteen-hundred-eleven-twelve that affluent rain had not descended.                                                          *Shirley*, I,1

He should have been a soldier, and circumstances had made him a priest. [Mr Helstone]                          *Ibid.*, I,3

'I sent them away, after arresting a rascal amongst them, whom I hope to transport – a fellow who preaches at the chapel yonder sometimes.' [Moses Barraclough]

(Robert Moore), *Ibid.*, I,9

The clergy were sacred beings in Miss Ainley's eyes; no matter what might be the insignificance of the individual, his station made him holy.

*Ibid.*, II,3

Britain would miss her church, if that church fell. God save it! God also reform it! *Ibid.*, II,5

The fat Dissenter who had given out the hymn was left sitting in the ditch. He was a spirit merchant by trade, a leader of the Nonconformists, and, it was said, drank more water in that one afternoon than he had swallowed for a twelvemonth before. *Ibid.*, II,6

Otherwise he was sane and rational, diligent and charitable. [Mr Macarthey]

*Ibid.*, III,14

I am sorry the Clergy do not like the doctrine of Universal Salvation.

Letter to Margaret Wooler, 14 February 1850

The Cardinal spoke in a smooth whining manner, just like a canting Methodist preacher. [Cardinal Wiseman]
Letter to Mr Brontë, 17 June 1851

'J'ai menti plusieurs fois' formed an item of every girl's and woman's monthly confession: the priest heard unshocked, and absolved unreluctant.

*Villette*, 9

There, as elsewhere, the CHURCH strove to bring up her children robust in body, feeble in soul, fat, ruddy, hale, joyous, ignorant, unthinking, unquestioning.

*Ibid.*, 14

Did I, do you suppose, reader, contemplate venturing
again within that worthy priest's reach? As soon should
I have thought of walking into a Babylonish furnace.

*Ibid.*, 15

It preached Romanism; it persuaded to conversion. The
voice of that sly little book was a honeyed voice; its
accents were all unction and balm.

*Ibid.*, 36

That a Priesthood might march straight on and straight
upward to an all-dominating eminence, whence they
might at last stretch the sceptre of their Moloch 'Church'.

*Ibid.*

# Religion

It may all die away, I may be in utter midnight, but I
implore a Merciful Redeemer that if this be the next
dawn of the Gospel, it may still brighten to perfect day.

Letter to Ellen Nussey, *c*. 1836

But the 'foretaste' passed away, and earth and sin
returned.            Letter to Ellen Nussey, 20 February 1837

'Do what you feel is right. Obey me, and even in the
sloughs of want I will plant for you firm footing.' And
then, as I walked fast along the road, there rose upon me
a strange, inly-felt idea of some Great Being, unseen, but
all-present, who in His beneficence desired only my
welfare and now watched the struggle of good and evil
in my heart, and waited to see whether I should obey.

*The Professor*, 20

'I hold another creed; which no one ever taught me, and
which I seldom mention; but in which I delight, and to
which I cling: for it extends hope to all: it makes Eternity
a rest – a mighty home, not a terror and an abyss.'

(Helen Burns), *Jane Eyre*, I,6

I care for myself. The more solitary, the more friendless,
the more unsustained I am, the more I will respect
myself. I will keep the law given by God; sanctioned by
man. I will hold to the principles received by me when I
was sane and not mad – as I am now.

*Ibid.*, III,1

We know that God is everywhere; but certainly we feel
His presence most when His works are on the grandest
scale spread before us; and it is in the unclouded
night-sky, where His worlds wheel their silent course,
that we read clearest His infinitude, His omnipotence,
His omnipresence.

*Ibid.*, III,2

'God had an errand for me; to bear which afar, to deliver
it well, skill and strength, courage and eloquence, the
best qualifications of soldier, statesman and orator, were
all needed: for these all centre in the good missionary.'

(St John Rivers), *Ibid.*, III,5

No fear of death will darken St John's last hour: his mind
will be unclouded; his heart will be undaunted; his hope
will be sure; his faith steadfast.

*Ibid.*, III,12

'The soul's real hereafter, who shall guess.'

(Caroline Helstone), *Shirley*, I,10

Her life came nearer the life of Christ than that of any
other human being he had ever met with. [Miss Ainley]

*Ibid.*

At moments she was a Calvinist, and, sinking into the
gulf of religious despair, she saw darkening over her the
doom of reprobation. [Caroline Helstone]

*Ibid.*, II,9

'Whom He loveth, He chasteneth.' These words are true,
and should not be forgotten.

*Ibid.*

For the rest, we are all in the hands of Him who
apportions His gifts.

Letter to Ellen Nussey, 18 July 1850

Some lives *are* thus blessed: it is God's will: it is the
attesting trace and lingering evidence of Eden.

*Villette*, 32

I am not a heathen, I am not hard-hearted, I am not
unchristian. I am not dangerous as they tell you; I would
not trouble your faith; you believe in God and Christ and
in the Bible, and so do I.

*Ibid.*, 35

That when I thought of sin and sorrow, of earthly
corruption, mortal depravity, weighty temporal woe – I
could not care for chanting priests or mumming officials.

*Ibid.*

Dark through the wilderness of this world stretches the
way for most of us: equal and steady be our tread; be our
cross our banner.

*Ibid.*, 37

# Reading

I am extremely glad that aunt has consented to take in 'Fraser's Magazine'.

Letter to Branwell, 17 May 1831

If you like poetry let it be first-rate; Milton, Shakespeare, Thomson, Goldsmith, Pope (if you will, though I don't admire him), Scott, Byron, Campbell, Wordsworth, and Southey. Now Ellen, don't be startled at the names of Shakespeare and Byron.

Letter to Ellen Nussey, 4 July 1834

'French and German works predominated – the old French dramatists, sundry modern authors, Thiers, Villemain, Paul de Kock, George Sand, Eugene Sue; in German – Goethe, Schiller, Zschokke, Jean Paul Richter; in English there were works on Political Economy.'

*The Professor*, 4

She had selected 'Paradise Lost' from her shelf of classics, thinking, I suppose, the religious character of the book best adapted it to Sunday. [Frances Henri]

*Ibid.*, 19

I frequently dosed her with Wordsworth in this way, and Wordsworth steadied her soon.

*Ibid.*, 25

Bessie asked if I would have a book: the word *book* acted as a transient stimulus, and I begged her to fetch 'Gulliver's Travels' from the library.

*Jane Eyre*, I,3

'Rasselas' looked dull to my trifling taste; I saw nothing about fairies, nothing about genii; no bright variety seemed spread over the closely-printed pages.

*Ibid.*, 1,5

A poem: one of those genuine productions so often vouchsafed to the fortunate public of those days – the golden age of modern literature. Alas! the readers of our era are less favoured. [*Marmion*]

*Ibid.*, III,6

It appears to me that Fielding's style is arid, and his views of life and human nature coarse, compared with Thackeray's.

Letter to W.S. Williams, 23 December 1847

Why do you like Miss Austen so very much?

Letter to G.H. Lewes, 12 January 1848

Miss Austen being, as you say, without 'sentiment', without *poetry*, maybe *is* sensible, real (more *real* than *true*), but she cannot be great.

Letter to G.H. Lewes, 18 January 1848

All is true in Thackeray.

Letter to W.S. Williams, 11 March 1848

We do not subscribe to a circulating library at Haworth, and consequently 'new novels' rarely indeed come in our way.

Letter to Ellen Nussey, 26 June 1848

'And Shakspeare is our science, since we are going to study.'

(Caroline Helstone), *Shirley*, 1,6

'I hope William Cowper is safe and calm in heaven now.'

(Caroline Helstone), *Ibid.*, II,1

'Was Rousseau ever loved?'

(Caroline Helstone), *Ibid.*

'Milton was great; but was he good?'

(Shirley Keeldar), *Ibid.*, II,7

It was a romance of Mrs Radcliffe's – 'The Italian'.

*Ibid.*, II,12

'You read French. Your mind is poisoned with French novels. You have imbibed French principles.' [Shirley Keeldar]

(Mr Sympson), *Ibid.*, III,8

Reading has, of late, been my great solace and recreation.

Letter to W.S. Williams, 13 September 1849

I have read none except 'Pride and Prejudice'.

Letter to W.S. Williams, 22 February 1850

Jane Austen was a complete and most sensible lady, but a very incomplete and rather insensible (*not senseless*) woman.

Letter to W.S. Williams, 12 April 1850

It is beautiful; it is mournful; it is monotonous. [*In Memoriam*]

Letter to Mrs Gaskell, 27 August 1850

'Wildfell Hall' it hardly appears to me desirable to preserve.

Letter to W.S. Williams, 5 September 1850

*Wuthering Heights* was hewn in a wild workshop, with simple tools out of homely materials.

Preface to *Wuthering Heights*, 1850

George Sand has a better nature than M. de Balzac.

Letter to G.H. Lewes, 17 October 1850

As usual, he is unjust to women, quite unjust. [Thackeray]

Letter to George Smith, 14 February 1852

Why are we to shut up the book weeping? [*Ruth*]

Letter to Mrs Gaskell, 26 April 1852

# Writing

There was a little girl and her name was Anne.

Juvenile Manuscript, c. 1827

I take advantage of the earliest opportunity to thank you
for the letter you favoured me with last week, and to
apologise for having so long neglected to write to you.

Letter to Ellen Nussey, 31 May 1831

> We wove a web in childhood,
> A web of sunny air;
> We dug a spring in infancy
> Of water pure and fair;

Poem, 19 December 1835

There is, reader, a sort of pleasure in sitting down to
write, wholly unprovided with a subject.

Juvenile Manuscript, 29 June 1837

I try to read, I try to write; but in vain.

Letter to Ellen Nussey, 15 November 1843

Gentlemen –
May I request to be informed whether you would
undertake the publication of a Collection of short poems
in one volume, oct.       Letter to Aylott & Jones, 28 January 1846

My narrative is not exciting, and above all, not
marvellous – but it may interest some individuals, who,
having toiled in the same vocation as myself, will find in
my experience frequent reflections of their own.

The Professor, 1

It appears to me that ambition – *literary* ambition
especially, is not a feeling to be cherished in the mind of
a woman.                                        (Mdlle Reuter), *Ibid.*, 18

Novelists should never allow themselves to weary of the
study of real life – If they observed this duty
conscientiously, they would give us fewer pictures
chequered with vivid contrasts of light and shade.

*Ibid.*, 19

Gentlemen –
C., E., and A. Bell are now preparing for the press a work
of fiction, consisting of three distinct and unconnected
tales, which may be published together, as a work of 3
vols. of the ordinary novel size, or separately as single
vols, as shall be deemed most advisable.

Letter to Aylott & Jones, 6 April 1846

Our book is found to be a drug, no man needs it or heeds
it. In the space of a year our publisher has disposed but
of two copies.

Letter to de Quincey, 16 June 1847

Mr Newby, however, does not do business like Messrs.
Smith & Elder.

Letter to W.S. Williams, 10 November 1847

Have you not two classes of writer – the author and the
bookmaker?

Letter to W.S. Williams, 15 February 1848

I have given *no one* a right either to affirm, or hint, in the
most distant manner, that I am 'publishing' – (humbug!)

Letter to Ellen Nussey, 3 May 1848

The first duty of an author is, I conceive, a faithful allegiance to Truth and Nature.

Letter to W.S. Williams, 14 August 1848

To such critics I would say, To you I am neither man nor woman – I come before you as an author only.

Letter to W.S. Williams, 16 August 1849

If you think, from this prelude, that anything like a romance is preparing for you, reader, you never were more mistaken.

*Shirley*, I

'But romance-writers might know nothing of love, judging by the way in which they treat of it.'

(Caroline Helstone), *Ibid.*, II,10

I have always felt certain that it is a deplorable error in an author to assume the tragic tone in advising the public about his own wrongs or griefs.

Letter to W.S. Williams, 31 August 1849

I must have my own way in the matter of writing.

Letter to W.S. Williams, 21 September 1849

In spite of all I have gone and done in the writing line, I still retained a place in her esteem. [Margaret Wooler]

Letter to Ellen Nussey, 16 February 1850

I cannot write books handling the topics of the day; it is of no use trying. Nor can I write a book for its moral.

Letter to George Smith, 30 October 1852

But stop – I must not, from the faithful narrator, degenerate into the partial eulogist.

*Villette*, 19

Arthur wishes you would burn my letters.

> Letter to Ellen Nussey, 7 November 1854

I am writing in haste. It is almost unexplicable to me that I seem so often hurried now.

> Letter to Ellen Nussey, 7 December 1854

I must write one line out of my weary bed.

> Letter to Ellen Nussey, 21 February 1855

# Nature

His eyes, which were fired with a flash of wild
enthusiasm, wandered over the sky, the sun, the river,
the smiling plains of his country.

*The Scrap Book*, 24 June 1835

Green, reedy swamps; fields fertile but flat, cultivated in
patches that made them look like magnified
kitchen-gardens; belts of cut trees, formal as pollard
willows, skirting the horizon; narrow canals, gliding
slow by the roadside; painted Flemish farm-houses;
some very dirty hovels; a gray dead sky; wet road, wet
fields, wet house-tops.

*The Professor*, 7

There was no possibility of taking a walk that day.

*Jane Eyre*, I,1

A ridge of lighted heath, alive, glancing, devouring,
would have been a meet emblem of my mind when I
accused and menaced Mrs Reed: the same ridge, black
and blasted after the flames are dead, would have
represented as meetly my subsequent condition, when
half an hour's silence and reflection had shown me the
madness of my conduct, and the dreariness of my hated
and hating position.

*Ibid.*, I,4

Leaning over the battlements and looking far down, I surveyed the grounds laid out like a map: the bright and velvet lawn closely girdling the grey base of the mansion; the field, wide as a park, dotted with its ancient timber; the wood, dun and sere, divided by a path visibly overgrown, greener with moss than the trees were with foliage; the church at the gates, the road, the tranquil hills, all reposing in the autumn day's sun; the horizon bounded by a propitious sky, azure, marbled with pearly white.                    *Ibid.*, I,11

The consequence was, that when the moon, which was full and bright (for the night was fine), came in her course to that space in the sky opposite my casement, and looked in at me through the unveiled panes, her glorious gaze roused me.                    *Ibid.*, II,5

'Mosquitoes came buzzing in and hummed sullenly round the room; the sea, which I could hear from thence, rumbled dull like an earthquake – black clouds were casting up over it; the moon was setting in the waves, broad and red, like a hot cannon-ball – she threw her last bloody glance over a world quivering with the ferment of tempest.'                    (Mr Rochester), *Ibid.*, III,1

There was a grass-grown track descending the forest aisle, between hoar and knotty shafts and under branched arches. I followed it, expecting soon to reach the dwelling; but it stretched on and on, it wound far and farther: no sign of habitation or grounds was visible.
                    *Ibid.*, III,11

He could walk miles on the most varying April day and never see the beautiful dallying of earth and heaven; never mark when a sunbeam kissed the hill-tops, making them smile clear in green light, or when a shower wept over them, hiding their crests with the low-hanging, dishevelled tresses of a cloud. [Mr Malone]
                    *Shirley*, I,2

'I have seen such storms in hilly districts in Yorkshire;
and at their riotous climax, while the sky was all
cataract, the earth all flood, I have remembered the
Deluge.'

(Shirley Keeldar), *Ibid.*, II,1


'I know certain lonely, quite untrodden glades, carpeted
with strange mosses, some yellow as if gilded, some a
sober gray, some gem-green.'

(Caroline Helstone), *Ibid.*


'I long to hear the sound of waves – ocean waves, and to
see them as I have imagined them in dreams, like tossing
banks of green light, strewed with vanishing and
reappearing wreaths of foam, whiter than lilies.'

(Caroline Helstone), *Ibid.*, II,2


Here he is, wandering alone, waiting duteously on
Nature, while she unfolds a page of stern, of silent, and
of solemn poetry beneath his attentive gaze. [Martin
Yorke]

*Ibid.*, III,9


I can tell, one summer evening, fifty years syne, my
mother coming running in just at edge of dark, almost
fleyed out of her wits, saying she had seen a fairish
[fairy] in Fieldhead Hollow; and that was the last fairish
that ever was seen in this countryside (though they've
been heard within these forty years). A lonesome spot it
was, and a bonny spot, full of oak trees and nut trees. It
is altered now.

*Ibid.*, III,14


The wind was wailing at the windows: it had wailed all
day; but as night deepened, it took a new tone – an
accent keen, piercing, almost articulate to the ear; a
plaint, piteous and disconsolate to the nerves, trilled in
every gust.

*Villette*, 4

Somewhat bare, flat, and treeless was the route along
which our journey lay; and slimy canals crept, like
half-torpid green snakes, beside the road; and formal
pollard willows edged level fields, tilled like
kitchen-garden beds.

*Ibid.*, 7

Arthur suggested the idea of the waterfall – after the
melted snow he said it would be fine. I had often wanted
to see it in its winter power, so we walked on. It was fine
indeed – a perfect torrent raving over the rocks white
and beautiful.

Letter to Ellen Nussey, 29 November 1854

# Art

A portrait-painter's sky (the most sombre and threatening of welkins) and distant trees of a conventional depth of hue raised in full relief a pale, pensive-looking female face, shadowed with soft dark hair, almost blending with the equally dark clouds; large solemn eyes looked reflectively into mine.

*The Professor*, 22

The two ships becalmed on a torpid sea, I believed to be marine phantoms.

The fiend pinning down the thief 's pack behind him, I passed over quickly: it was an object of terror.

So was the black horned thing seated aloof on a rock, surveying a distant crowd surrounding a gallows.

Each picture told a story.

*Jane Eyre*, I,1

One gleam of light lifted into relief a half-submerged mast, on which sat a cormorant, dark and large, with wings flecked with foam; its beak held a gold bracelet set with gems, that I had touched with as brilliant tints as my palette could yield, and as glittering distinctness as my pencil could impart.

*Ibid.*, I,13

Draw in chalk your own picture, faithfully; without softening one defect: omit no harsh line, smooth away no displeasing irregularity; write under it, 'Portrait of a Governess, disconnected, poor, and plain.'

*Ibid.*, II,1

Afterwards, take a piece of smooth ivory – you have one prepared in your drawing-box: take your palette, mix your freshest, finest, clearest tints; choose your most delicate camel-hair pencils; delineate carefully the loveliest face you can imagine.

*Ibid.*

One morning I fell to sketching a face: what sort of a face it was to be, I did not care or know.

*Ibid.*, II,6

Thackeray may not be a painter, but he is a wizard of a draughtsman; touched with his pencil, paper lives.

Letter to W.S. Williams, 11 March 1848

'Come, child, you are always stooping over palette, or book, or sampler; leave that tinting work. By-the-by, do you put your pencil to your lips when you paint?'

(Mr Helstone on Caroline Helstone), *Shirley*, I,11

She was compared with the heiress, as a graceful pencil sketch compared with a vivid painting. [Caroline Helstone and Shirley Keeldar]

*Ibid.*, II,2

Nothing charmed me more during my stay in Town than the pictures I saw.

Letter to Margaret Wooler, 14 February 1850

All these four 'Anges' were grim and grey as burglars, and cold and vapid as ghosts. What women to live with! insincere, ill-humoured, bloodless, brainless nonentities! As bad in their way as the indolent gipsy-giantess, the Cleopatra, in hers.

*Villette*, 19

It was a marvellous sight: a mighty revelation.
It was a spectacle low, horrible, immoral.

*Ibid.*, 23

Place now the Cleopatra, or any other slug, before her as
an obstacle, and see her cut through the pulpy mass as
the scimitar of Saladin clove the down cushion.

*Ibid.*

# Death

Aunt, Martha Taylor and Mr Weightman are now all gone; how dreary and void everything seems.

Letter to Ellen Nussey, 10 November 1842

Mr Reed had been dead nine years: it was in this chamber he breathed his last; here he lay in state; hence his coffin was borne by the undertaker's men; and since that day, a sense of dreary consecration had guarded it from frequent intrusion.

*Jane Eyre*, I,2

Her grave is in Brocklebridge churchyard: for fifteen years after her death it was only covered by a grassy mound; but now a grey marble tablet marks the spot, inscribed with her name, and the word 'Resurgam'.

*Ibid.*, I,9

There was stretched Sarah Reed's once robust and active frame, rigid and still: her eye of flint was covered with its cold lid; her brow and strong traits wore yet the impress of her inexorable soul.

*Ibid.*, II,6

'We have buried our dead out of our sight.' [Branwell]

Letter to W.S. Williams, 2 October 1848

I felt, as I had never felt before that there was peace and forgiveness for him in heaven. [Branwell]

Letter to W.S. Williams, 6 October 1848

Emily suffers no more from pain or weakness. She will never suffer more in this world.

Letter to Ellen Nussey, 23 December 1848

My darling, thou wilt never know
The grinding agony of woe
That we have borne for thee.
Thus may we consolation tear
E'en from the depth of our despair
And wasting misery.

Poem, 24 December 1848


Emily is nowhere here now – her wasted mortal remains are taken out of the house.

Letter to W.S. Williams, 25 December 1848


With almost her last breath she said she was happy and thanked God that death has come, and come so gently. [Anne]

Letter to W.S. Williams, 30 May 1849


Here is the place – green sod and a gray marble headstone – Jessy sleeps below. She lived through an April day; much loved was she, much loving.

*Shirley*, I,9


More than one deep crimson stain was visible on the gravel; a human body lay quiet on its face near the gates: and five or six wounded men writhed and moaned in the bloody dust.

*Ibid.*, II,8


Jessie lay cold, coffined, solitary – only the sod screening her from the storm.

*Ibid.*, II,12


Not always do those who dare such divine conflict prevail.

*Ibid.*, III,2

The night passed in quietness; quietly her doom must at
last have come: peacefully and painlessly: in the
morning she was found without life, nearly cold, but all
calm and undistorted. [Miss Marchmont]

*Villette*, 4

Peace, be still! Oh! a thousand weepers, praying in
agony on waiting shores, listened for that voice, but it
was not uttered – not uttered till, when the hush came,
some could not feel it: till, when the sun returned, his
light was night to some!

*Ibid.*, 42

# Other Brontës

## Anne

I am a governess in the family of Mr Robinson. I dislike
the situation and wish to change it for another.

Diary Paper, 30 July 1841

All true histories contain instruction.

Agnes Grey, 1

I am your child's mother, and your housekeeper –
nothing more.

(Helen Huntingdon on Arthur Huntingdon)<br>The Tenant of Wildfell Hall, II,14

'But thank God I have hope – not only from a vague
dependence on the possibility that penitence and pardon
might have reached him at the last, but from the blessed
confidence that, though whatever purging fires the
erring spirit may be doomed to pass – whatever fate
awaits it, still, it is not lost, and God, who hateth nothing
that he hath made, will bless it in the end.'

(Helen Huntingdon), Ibid., III,12

A dreadful darkness closes in
On my bewildered mind;
O let me suffer and not sin,
Be tortured yet resigned.

Poem, 7 January 1849

### Branwell

Who finds no Heaven beyond life's gloomy skies
Who sees no Hope to brighten up that gloom
Tis *He* who feels the worm that never dies
The *Real* death and darkness of the tomb

Poem, 14 May 1842

I shall be very much obliged to you if you can contrive to
get me Five pence worth of Gin in a proper measure.

Letter to John Brown, 1848

### Emily

Cold in the earth, and fifteen wild Decembers
From those brown hills have melted into spring –
Faithful indeed is the spirit that remembers
After such years of change and suffering!

Poem, 3 March 1845

Strike it down – that other boughs may flourish
Where that perished sapling used to be;
Thus, at least, its mouldering corpse will nourish
That from which it sprung – Eternity.

Poem, 10 April 1845

Tabby has just been teasing me to turn as formerly to
'Pilloputate'.

Diary entry, 30 July 1845

Then dawns the Invisible, the Unseen its truth
    reveals;
My outward sense is gone, my inward essence feels:
Its wings are almost free – its home, its harbour
    found;
Measuring the gulf it stoops and dares the final
    bound.

Poem, 9 October 1845

No coward soul is mine,
No trembler in the world's storm-troubled sphere;
I see Heaven's glories shine
And Faith shines equal arming me from Fear.

Poem, 2 January 1846

'It would degrade me to marry Heathcliff, now; so he
shall never know how I love him; and that, not because
he's handsome, Nelly, but because he's more myself than
I am.'

(Catherine Earnshaw), *Wuthering Heights*, I,9

'Nelly, I *am* Heathcliff '

(Catherine Earnshaw), *Ibid.*

Two words would comprehend my future, death and
hell: existence after losing her would be hell.

(Heathcliff), *Ibid.*, I,14

'She showed herself, as she often was in life, a devil to
me! And, since then, sometimes more and sometimes
less, I've been the sport of that intolerable torture!'

(Heathcliff), *Ibid.*, II,15

I lingered round them, under that benign sky, watched
the moths fluttering among the heath and hare-bells;
listened to the soft wind breathing through the grass;
and wondered how any one could ever imagine unquiet
slumbers for the sleepers in that quiet earth.

(Lockwood), *Ibid.*, II,20

### Mrs Brontë

My dear saucy Pat ...

Letter, 18 November 1812

Taking this vow of poverty, where are the evils
attending it?

Manuscript, *c.* 1815

### Mr Brontë

With a horrible din,
Afflictions may swell
They cleanse me from sin,
They save me from hell

Poem, published 1811

The world with all its pains, pleasures, fears and hopes will soon have an end; but an eternity of unutterable happiness or misery is the grand characteristick of the next world.

Letter to Miss Burder, 1 January 1824